DATE DUE

OCT 5 1989		
SEP 7 - 1993		
MAR 2 - 1994		
MAR 29 1997		
MAR 1 3 2001		
AUG 0 6 1997		
JUN 0 1 2011		

FAFNIR

MONSTERS OF MYTHOLOGY

25 VOLUMES

Hellenic

Amycus
Anteus
The Calydonian Boar
Cerberus
Chimaera
The Cyclopes
The Dragon of Boeotia
The Furies
Geryon
Harpalyce
Hecate
The Hydra
Ladon
Medusa
The Minotaur
The Nemean Lion
Procrustes
Scylla and Charybdis
The Sirens
The Spear-birds
The Sphinx

Norse

Fafnir
Fenris

Celtic

Drabne of Dole
Pig's Ploughman

MONSTERS OF MYTHOLOGY

FAFNIR

Bernard Evslin

CHELSEA HOUSE PUBLISHERS

New York   Philadelphia

1989

EDITOR
Remmel Nunn

ART DIRECTOR
Maria Epes

PICTURE RESEARCHER
Susan Quist

SENIOR DESIGNER
Marjorie Zaum

EDITORIAL ASSISTANTS
Heather Lewis, Mark Rifkin

First Printing

1 3 5 7 9 8 6 4 2

Library of Congress Cataloging-in-Publication Data

Evslin, Bernard.
Fafnir / Bernard Evslin

p.   cm.—(Monsters of mythology)
Summary: Recounts the myth of Fafnir, the shape-shifting ogre
whose thirst for destruction led him into a violent confrontation
with the Germanic hero Siegfried.
ISBN 1-55546-247-2
1. Fafnir (Germanic mythology)—Juvenile literature. [1. Fafnir
(Germanic mythology) 2. Siegfried (Legendary character)
3. Mythology, Germanic.] I. Title. II. Series: Evslin, Bernard.
Monsters of mythology.
BL670.F28E97   1989   398.2′1′09363—dc19
88-27110   CIP   AC

Printed in Singapore

For Mick the Quick, AKA Monica
Evslin—so that she may be induced
to read at least one of my
collected works

Contents

Characters

Monsters

Fafnir
(FAFF nuhr)
A vicious ogre who can assume the form of many creatures; dragon is his deadliest mode

Hreidmar
(RIDE mahr)
Fafnir's father, a prominent ogre

Oter
(AHT ehr)
Fafnir's hungry, shape-shifting brother

Regnir
(REGG neer)
Fafnir's eldest brother, a misshapen dwarf who is extremely cunning, murderously greedy, and an adept magician

Gods

Odin
(OHD in)
King of the Gods, all-powerful within the bonds of fate

Frigga
(FRIGG uh)
Odin's eldest wife, Queen of the Gods

Loki (LOH kee)	A renegade giant adopted by the Gods, a favorite of Odin's; the arch-trickster, fiendishly clever and totally treacherous
Thor (THORR)	The God of Thunder, Lord of the Hammer
Urd (UHRD)	Eldest Norn, spinner of the Fatal Web
Skuld (SKUHLD)	The second of the Norn sisters
Verdandi (vehr DAHN dee)	The third of the Norn sisters
Arla (AHR luh)	Eldest of the Rhine-maidens, beautiful river nymphs descended from God and Giantess
Dure (DOOR eh)	Arla's sister
Helge (HEHL geh)	Youngest of the Rhine-maidens

Mortals

Siegfried (SIG freed)	A young hero, last of the Valsungs
Sigmund (SIG muhnd)	Siegfried's father, a mighty warrior
The Princess	Sigmund's wife, Siegfried's mother

Others

Smith Dwarfs	Magical metal workers whose smithy is a crater

FAFNIR

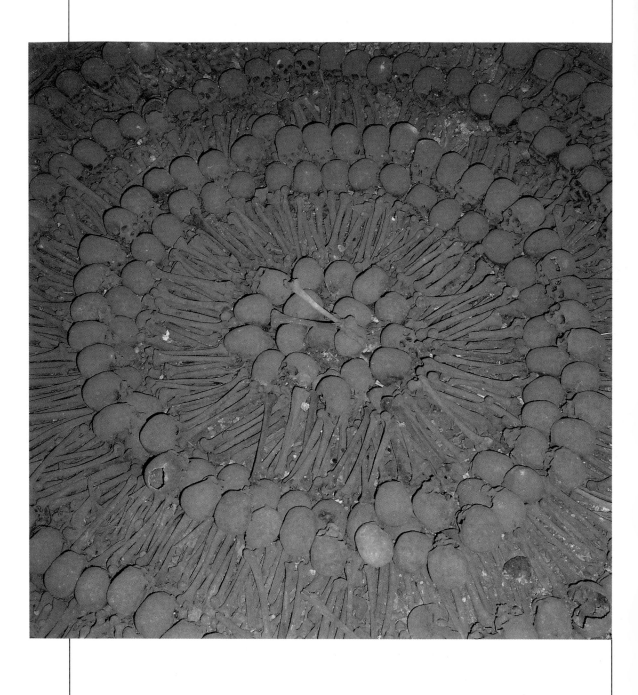

1

The Ogres' Den

n a clearing in a deep, dark forest stood a house where no one came who didn't live there or wasn't dragged there. At first sight it looked like a sprawling white lodge made of shells, but on second look you could see that they were not shells but bones. The front door was an archway formed by the pelvis bone of a giant. Straight shin bones and arm bones were the wall struts. The heavy beams were made of thigh bones. The roof, which had to be strong enough to bear the weight of an entire winter's snowfall, was made of overlapping shoulder bones.

As for skulls, they were used for drinking cups, bowls, flowerpots, according to size—which ranged from giant to dwarf, with a lot of plain human skulls, adult and child.

Anyone unlucky enough to be looking at this bone house knew that it had to be the home of something dreadful, and that unless he left the neighborhood immediately he would find himself being boiled alive in a big iron pot, or else eaten raw.

Indeed, a gruesome clan did live there, the ogre Hreidmar and his three sons, Oter, Regnir, and Fafnir. Hreidmar's father had been an arch-demon, too ferocious even for the god-hating, man-devouring Giants of Jutenheim, who had driven him out of their land, banishing him forever. He had then married the ugliest daughter of the ugliest gnome of the tribe of Dismal Dwarfs—and this gnarled maiden, although horrible to look at, was also very magical. The grisly pair produced a son named Hreidmar, who began planning their murder when he was nine days old, and killed them as soon as he was big enough to use a knife.

Hreidmar grew with monstrous speed and raided Jutenheim, stealing himself a wife, who bore him three sons. Then, knowing that Hreidmar meant to kill her and take a fresh young wife, she fled the bone house and made her way back to Jutenheim, leaving her husband and three children.

But Hreidmar was resolved that his sons would not do to him as he had done to his own parents. He flogged them twice a day when they were good and all day long if they weren't. He twisted their ears, crimped their noses, and tormented them in other ways, hoping to fill them with such wholesome terror that they wouldn't dare think of attacking him.

After a time, however, he realized that he would have to change his methods because he could no longer hurt his sons. He had lost none of his monstrous vigor; he was as strong as ever and could slice the bough off a tree with one flick of his whip, but his sons had grown the scaly hide of true Ogres and his lash could no longer cut them. So he decided to try kindness, hoping he would know how, and that it wasn't too late.

Regnir, the eldest, said to him, "Glad you've come to your senses, Father. You're safe with us. We don't mean to harm you. We want you to teach us magic."

Whereupon Hreidmar taught them all he knew about the dark arts—shape changing, invisibility, harms and charms, dream reading, and how to brew ten poisons from one innocent-looking herb garden.

Curiously enough, Regnir, who resembled his Dismal Dwarf grandmother and was much the cleverest of his family, was the only one who could not learn to transform himself. He

Hreidmar taught his sons all he knew about the
dark arts—shape changing, invisibility,
harms and charms, dream reading. . . .

tried and tried but could never become a wolf, a fox, a bear, or any of the beautiful, lithe animal shapes the others wore so easily. He made himself adept at all the other kinds of magic, but decided to hide his skills. Being so much the smallest of his clan, he depended on stealth and cunning to keep things even. Indeed, he thought so fast and spoke so well that the others began to look on him as their leader.

And they needed fast thinking at this point, for they had begun to rob their neighbors full-time.

Working as a team, father and sons raided all the farms the country round and helped themselves to sleek herds of cattle before killing the owners. Their barnyard became a slaughter pen. They collected so many bones they decided to build another house and two more barns.

For all their teamwork, though, the brothers secretly hated each other, and all of them loathed their father—who, also secretly, feared and hated them. But that was the way of close-knit ogre families, and still is.

Now all three of the young ogres were savagely greedy, but with different greeds. Regnir lusted for gold, believing that with enough of it he could buy whatever else he might want. He loved the yellow metal, however, not only for what it could buy, but for itself. The chink of gold against gold was sweetest music to him, its rich gleam the most gorgeous sight in the whole world. He knew that his father, who had looted the entire countryside, was very wealthy, and Regnir intended to inherit this wealth as soon as he could, and to be the sole heir. For this to happen, three deaths had to happen first, but he was more than ready to arrange fatalities.

In Oter, the second son, burned the simplest hunger—for food. He was always famished, and the more he ate, the more he wanted. As soon as he learned to change shape, he became a hawk, for he had observed that birds eat all day long, and that the hawk was the most successful of all hunting birds. As a hawk, he prowled the sky, diving upon other birds, seizing them in his claws, stripping flesh from bone, and eating everything except beak and feathers.

Overflying a river one day, he spotted a bear scooping salmon out of the rushing water and devouring them from nose to tail. The delicious smell of the fish drifted up to him, and he was immediately gripped by a raging hunger for salmon. No bird could satisfy him now, no rabbit, lamb, or kid or anything that hawks hunted. What he wanted was salmon, and they were un-catchable by hawks. Hovering over the river, he observed that while a bear could catch many salmon by squatting at the side of a stream and scooping them out with his paw, there was

As a hawk, Oter prowled the sky . . .

another animal that could actually swim like a fish and could catch more salmon in an hour than a bear could in a day. It was a sleek, swift animal whose rolling muscles were clad in oiled fur. Its hind feet were webbed, its front paws as clever as hands.

In a flash, Oter changed himself into that beast, plunged into the river and ate so many salmon so fast that the entire tribe watched him in wonder, and took his name, calling themselves *otters*.

As for the third son, Fafnir, his keenest delight was in making others fear him. Being the youngest of the family, he had been the smallest for some years, and had been made to suffer for it. Every time one of the brothers was flogged by his father he would fling himself upon Fafnir, punching and kicking him until he slumped, senseless, to the ground. If both brothers were beaten by their father, they would both attack Fafnir. He soon learned to curl up like a hedgehog under attack. When he did this, his brothers would use him like a ball, kicking him from one to the other in the world's first soccer game. And when this punishment was finished, his father would beat him again for not standing up to his attackers.

But Fafnir absorbed what was dealt out to him and was toughened by it. He grew much faster than his brothers, and in a few years was the largest and strongest of the family. By this time, of course, his brothers considered it wiser not to bully him.

But the cruelty Fafnir had absorbed made him even more vicious than the rest of his clan, which was very difficult to be. And so the appetite that burned in him was to make others afraid. He snuffled up the odor of fear like the most delicious musk, drank tears like wine, and enjoyed nothing more than the sight of someone groveling and writhing underfoot as he leered down, promising his victim that, as a last favor, he would lengthen his life by killing him slowly.

He enjoyed killing in his own shape, but when facing a genuine Jutenheim giant or a magic-wielding dwarf, or some other who might not be impressed by his ogreish size, he chose a shape that would strike terror in anyone: an enormous weasel that could devour a bull, say, as easily as an ordinary weasel consumes a squirrel. Or he would become a gigantic scorpion with a sting as big as a plough, or change himself into a vampire bat with a wingspread greater than an eagle's—who could suck a villageful of people dry of blood in a single night.

This was Fafnir, youngest ogre, and most monstrous. But all the blood he drank, all the bones he crunched, all the delicious terror he kindled only made him want more and more and more. Somewhere, he sensed, there existed a creature even more terrible than an outsize weasel or scorpion or bat. He didn't know what it might be, but knew he had to become it. And for every day and night that passed before he could assume that final shape of horror, he would make others pay in pain and suffering.

2

Odin's Gold

ods and Giants were cousins. They all sprang out of the wastes of chaos when fire and ice mixed explosively into crude blobs of something *Wholly New*. And out of these wondrous blobs had clotted the shapes of God and Giant. Now, Giant was the first shape and had sopped up certain crudities that made that tribe bigger and stronger and more brutal than the Gods—who had refined themselves out of the first blobs and made each other out of the finest essences of fire and ice.

Now, thousands of years later but still early in the world's morning, the Gods in their sky-pasture of Aesgard were an awesomely stunning tribe, fiercely beautiful as the changing seasons. Odin, their king, wore a beard that looked like spun snow. Freya's skin was snow-white overlaid with the blush of the northern rose; her eyes were blue as the core of flame. Indeed, all the Aesgir had blue eyes, except for Thor, Lord of Battle, whose eyes were smouldering coals. His hair and beard were fire-red. His grip on his war hammer like the clench of December that stills the wild northern seas. Balder the Good had eyes like the washed blue of sky after storm; his laughter was the pure sound of rivers in May slipping their fetters of ice. While the love goddess, Freya, walked in a fragrance that held the furious sweetness of rose and lilac and privet—who know how brief their summer is, how swiftly they must scent the air and fill the pouches of bees with nectar.

Intertwined with nature as they were, the Gods were weather-makers. When angry, Odin shook blizzards out of his snow-beard. Thor's war chariot rumbling across the sky was thunder. The sparks struck by his hammer against the helmet of a Giant was lightning. Frigga, Odin's jealous wife, when angry with her husband, which was often, spat tempests upon the earth.

But the worst weather of all was the boredom of Odin.

Frigga, Odin's jealous wife,
when angry with her husband, which was often,
spat tempests upon the earth.

Then his wild restlessness filled the sky and tormented the earth with wind-driven snow, hailstones as big as goose eggs, and weird winter lightning. At such times even the Gods trembled, for they were afraid that the storm of Odin's mood would kill all the people of earth, leaving no one to worship them. And Gods, unworshiped, lose their beauty and wither into monsters. As it happened, the thing that bored Odin most was fighting with his wife, even when he won. And they were quarreling now.

"I shall weep," hissed Frigga. "I shall howl. I shall wait until you're asleep and do painful things to you."

"You seem displeased, my dear," murmured Odin. "Any reason?"

"Any reason?" she screeched. "Don't you think I could see you in that river down there, sporting with those yellow-haired hussies?"

"They're all blonde in this part of the world, my queen. For dark-haired ones I'd have to go farther south."

"You're laughing at me!" she yowled, and sprang toward him, talons bared, trying to scratch his eyes out. He caught her wrists in one hand, swung her off her feet and set her on a bevel of the small star that was used to light the Royal Garden at Aesgard. She tried to clamber down but he slapped the star, making it spin on its axis. She clung desperately, crying:

"Let me down! Let me down!"

"No. You shall stay up there until you come to your senses."

"What were you doing in that river, you shameless lout?"

"As a matter of fact," said Odin, "I was preparing something splendid for you. I can't tell you what because it's meant to be a surprise."

"You'd better tell me," said Frigga. "I think what you're preparing is an enormous lie, but I'm listening."

"Well, you may have forgotten, but our thousandth anniversary is approaching. And to celebrate our glorious marriage

I've had the Delving Dwarfs digging into the earth all year long, piling up a hoard of gold that is my gift to you. Now, so rich a trove will tempt all the thievish Giants and Ogres and Dismal Dwarfs in our domain. So I mean to hide the gold in a river cave and have appointed those three maidens you saw to guard it. When you spotted me I was testing how well they swim and dive and so forth, and instructing them in their duties."

"A magnificent lie, husband," said Frigga. "Even by your standards. One worthy of Loki himself."

"You don't believe me?"

"What kind of an idiot do you take me for? Why would anyone choose creatures like these to guard a treasure against Giants and Ogres and such?"

"Because," said Odin, "it has been ordained that no one can steal that gold unless he foreswears love forever. Now, you have seen those sisters. Would you not describe them as gorgeous?"

"Only if my taste were as coarse as yours."

"Let me assure you, wife, that no one, and I mean no male at all, finding himself among those wet beauties, could force himself to foreswear the pleasures of love, no matter how greedy he was for gold. Yes, Frigga, they will guard the golden hoard. No thief shall be able to get past them to steal my gift to you. And on our anniversary day you shall cast off your suspicions and admit that I'm the superbly generous and affectionate husband I've always claimed to be."

Frigga grunted and fell silent. And Odin was swept by a wild restlessness.

"Send for Loki!" he bellowed.

"Loki!" shrieked Frigga. "Didn't you promise you'd never invite that troublemaker back to Aesgard?"

"Consider the promise broken," said Odin. "And I'd strongly advise you not to question anything I choose to do or I may do something you'll like even less."

"Are you threatening me?"

*"Why would anyone choose creatures like these to guard a
treasure against Giants and Ogres
and such?" asked Frigga.*

"Yes. Now get out of my sight, and while you're there
send someone for Loki. Understand?"

"More than you ever will," she muttered, but not loud
enough for him to hear, and hurried away. As eldest wife she
held permanent nagging rights, but no one ever dared provoke
Odin's full wrath.

"My whole family hates Loki," said Odin to himself. "Indeed, they have reason; he's always trying to do someone a mis-
chief. It's his nature, I suppose. Nevertheless, he's as witty as he
is treacherous, and the only one who can think of things to divert
me when I feel this way."

So Loki was sent a message, summoning him to Aesgard.
As it happened, however, he had received an earlier invitation to
visit the Norns—something that no one, except Odin himself,
would think of ignoring.

3

The Fatal Web

The Norns dwelt above the northern rim of the great slope of sky that was Aesgard. Their home was a vast tent made of black sheepskin that loomed like a storm cloud over the fleecy turrets of the god-castles. Indeed, the very existence of these dread sisters known as Norns cast a shadow over every life being lived on earth, or above it, or beneath it.

They struck fear into everyone—except Odin, who feared nothing—and in him they excited hatred and disgust. He hated the Norns because they were the only creatures in the world who could sometimes stop him from doing what he wanted to do, and they disgusted him because they were so ugly. Lover of beauty as he was, especially female beauty, the merest glimpse of these hideous sisters could send him into spasms of loathing.

They were hags with hairy faces and popping eyes. Their bodies were round as chariot wheels and studded with arms and legs, three of each. Scuttling on these arms and legs they would glide up the walls and spin webs—each web as big as the mainsail of a Viking ship. When the webs were spun they would open their snag-toothed mouths and sing a magic rune, the first song ever sung: *The Song of That-to-Be, Sung by All Three.*

At the end of the song, Urd, the chief sister, would fling a handful of lentils into the air; each lentil became a fly. But these were not ordinary flies. Most of them wore human faces. Some of them, the larger ones, wore the faces of Giants, and Ogres, and Dismal Dwarfs—who were smaller than Giants or Ogres, but bigger than humans.

The flies buzzed about, swerving in the air, trying to dodge the webs. Each minute in the Tent of Fate was a half year in human time. But the strands of the web were so fine they were almost invisible, and the spider sisters could shift them swiftly, trapping their prey in midair. One by one the flies landed in a web, were wrapped in silk, and devoured. And each time one was eaten, whoever wore that face on earth, or under earth, or in Jutenheim, died.

The flies with human faces all landed in the webs of Skuld or Verdandi. Urd's web, the largest, held the Giants and the Ogres, the Dwarfs and the Gnomes. One by one she wrapped them in silk and ate them, and sucked the marrow out of their bones, leaving only dry splinters clinging to the web. She almost filled her fat gut, but still had room for more.

"Aieee!" she howled to herself. "One day I'll be able to take Gods into my net. What a splendid feast I'll have then. Not yet. Not yet. Soon perhaps, but not yet. For they are still immortal and have not yet been taught to die. But I'll teach them. They shall learn. They are stubborn and slow to learn but I am stubborn too, and very patient."

She motioned to her sisters, who stopped spinning their webs and came to her. She said:

"Sisters mine, we are about to weave a great design—wherein will cross and recross the fates of the arrogant Gods and obnoxious Heroes, forbidden treasures and dire quests, high crimes and stupid generosities, imperiled maidens and doomed rescues. And Giants galore and Ogres aplenty; Dismal Dwarfs and a fine selection of monsters. And the last panel in our tapestry will be a gloriously bloody battle raging across the arch of heavens between Aesgard and Jutenheim. Aye, sisters, the sunset of this age will be the blood of the Gods spilling across the horizon. Enmeshed in our design, Odin and his loathsome tribe will pay for past privilege with their very lives."

"But the Gods are immortal," said Skuld. "How can they die?"

"A very good question," said Urd, "—that has a wonderfully bad answer. And that answer shall be revealed as we weave our design, the first stitch of which will be today's guest, black-hearted, orange-haired Loki."

"We don't understand," said Skuld and Verdandi together.

"You will . . . you will. Now back to work, my dears. As we sit here chatting, neglecting our webs, people are living too long, saddening their heirs."

The two younger hags scuttled up the walls and took up their webs where they had left off. Urd turned to greet Loki, who had just entered.

"Hail, great Norn," he said. "How may I serve you?"

"It is I who shall serve you this day, my son. Is there nothing you wish to ask of one who has so much to give?"

"Oh, yes, yes," said Loki. "I don't know where to start. I want everything of value anyone else happens to possess."

"A good start," said Urd. "A bit modest. . . . But I can offer you something even sweeter."

"What could that be?"

"Vengeance."

"Against whom?"

"Against him whom you hate the most in the world. We shall not utter his name, but you know who it is, and I know it. For I can read your secret thoughts."

"I am all attention, wise and powerful Urd."

"Harken, Loki," said Urd. "For you a glorious destiny is being designed. You, who were born a Giant of Jutenheim and

despise your kin, you who are a guest of the Gods and loathe
your hosts—you, Loki, perpetual stranger, clown, trickster, arch-
traitor, it is you who shall drag the Gods down from their high
places. You who are Odin's toady shall be Odin's doom."

"How?" whispered Loki. "How?"

"Shall I teach you how?"

"No! I shan't listen. This is some trick to destroy me. How
can I be the doom of one who is immortal?"

"You shall strip him of his immortality."

"That is beyond my power, or your power, or anyone's.
He is King of the Gods who are all immortal, and he the most."

"You are right, Loki, you clever one. No one can strip
Odin of his immortality, except . . ."

"Except?"

"Except Odin himself."

"Why should he do that?"

"You shall persuade him. Does he not depend upon you to
ease his boredom, to show him fresh pleasures?"

"He does, occasionally."

"Occasionally is enough. You shall use his own nature
against him—his restlessness, his curiosity, his courage."

"Easy to say, hard to do. Odin may favor me from time
to time, but the favor of kings, as you know, is most unreliable.
Besides, he is surrounded by those who loathe the sight of me.
Frigga, his wife, hisses when I approach, arches her back like a
great cat, seems to grow talons. . . . Thor, that murderous brute,
his red-furred fingers tighten on his hammer as soon as he sees
me. Once he actually threw it at me; it passed so close the wind
of its going knocked me down."

"Don't you want to do as I ask?" said Urd very softly.

"I want to, yes. But I'm afraid. I'm afraid."

"You don't yet know what fear is. Observe that large fly
up there."

"That one?"

"Yes. Notice anything strange about him?"

"Observe that fly up there. . . .
Notice anything strange about him?"

"He seems to be wearing a woolly orange wig. And his eyes . . . they're yellow. It's me! He's wearing a mask of my face!"

"And now," said Urd, "I cast a strand of my web thus. He is snared—thus. I approach—so . . . my next move will be to wrap him swiftly in silk, and eat him slowly. As I do this, Loki, you will feel the fangs of death entering your own gut, and will die, cursing your fate."

"Don't eat him, Urd. Please!"

"But I will—unless . . ."

"Unless I do as you say? Is that what you mean?"

"Exactly what I mean. But if you obey me, I shall let him fly free. And he will fall into no web of mine until The End of All Things. Obey me in this, trick Odin into yielding the shield of his immortality, and you shall outlive him and all the Gods. And everyone else on earth, or beneath it, or above it. Everyone, in fact, except me."

"Great Urd, your will shall be performed. But, I pray, give me a hint how to proceed."

"Come here. Let me whisper. This is the deepest, darkest, most dangerous secret in the universe. I don't even want my sisters to hear . . ."

4

The Trickster

eading from the Norns' black tent to Aesgard was a span of intertwined icicles. And this ice was so cold it stayed unmelted even by the summer sun. But the sun did melt the surface of the icy bridge, making it very slick. And Loki, skipping out of the Norns' gloomy den into a blaze of sunlight, slid gleefully all the way to Aesgard. He rushed to the cloud castle but was met by Odin outside the gates. One look told him that the King of the Gods was in a very ugly mood.

"Where have you been?" roared Odin. "I sent for you hours ago."

"Oh pardon, my master, but no message reached me. I was summoned by Urd this morning and have spent half a day in the tent of the Norns."

"What did the old bitch want?"

"I'm not sure," said Loki. "She made me observe how they spin their foul webs and decree their daily dooms. Then she mumbled a string of warnings at me—so many that I lost track of what she was talking about. I think she wanted to frighten me for some reason. But I'm here now, sire. And at your service."

"I'm bored, Loki, hideously bored. Not a torpor, mind

you. I'm boiling with restlessness. I feel that I might tear the sky apart. Perhaps I'll start with the tent of the Norns."

"I've been thinking about you, my lord," said Loki. "In fact, I think of little else but how best to serve you. And I believe I may have discovered the key to your dissatisfaction."

"Speak!"

"Of all the qualities of life, you admire courage the most. Yet you are forbidden to exercise it."

"What do you mean?"

"Look down upon Midgard, Master, and observe men and women as they lead their daily lives."

Odin looked down upon earth and its seven seas. It was summertime, and men had gone a-viking. He picked out one

Odin looked down upon earth and its seven seas.
It was summertime, and men had gone a-viking.

crew of yellow-haired, yellow-bearded men who had launched their vessel, and, having raised their single sail, were riding the wind over huge swells. The wind was astern now, but when it shifted, Odin knew, they would drop sail, unship their long oars, and row across hundreds of miles of broken water. And these northern seas could be almost as stormy in summer as in winter. The Vikings had slung their shields over the coaming; the ship wore the targes like a necklace. Swords and spears and battle-axes were wrapped carefully in oiled cloth.

"Observe them," said Loki, "as their tiny splinter of a ship crawls across the vast, implacable sea. Nor do they consider such a voyage anything to brag about. Real peril, they know, will begin when they hit shore. For they sail in search of booty— which means they will raid another coast, strike inland, hurl themselves upon forces many times their number, seize treasure and slaves, and put out to sea again. And by this time, perhaps, winter will have set in, and ice-fanged gales will savage them as they make the long voyage home."

Odin nodded wordlessly and turned his gaze toward shore. There he saw embattled men, and women too—for the tall northern women often fought alongside their men. He watched them hunting or being hunted. Watched them fighting, winning, losing. Watched as they farmed the earth and fished the sea, bore their young and buried their dead. He returned to the Viking crew and studied their faces, noted their look of grim joy.

"Well, my lord," said Loki, "how do they look to you?"

"Some look glad, some look sad. None of them look bored. Is that what you wanted me to see?"

"Yes," said Loki. "And the lesson these earthlings can teach us who live on high is the value of risk."

Odin's eye raked Loki's face, but he said nothing.

"Yes, *risk*!" cried Loki. "Utter risk! Life grows most precious when most threatened. Then, every filament glows. The endangered one plunders each hour of its possibilities like a bee looting a rose."

*Odin turned his gaze toward shore as humans
farmed the earth, bore their young
and buried their dead.*

"You grow strangely eloquent, Loki."

"Ah, my king, I must tell you that man, that lesser breed, enjoys himself in a way that the Gods will never know."

"Let us change ourselves into men, then, and seek adventure."

"Useless, my lord. It won't work."

"Why not?" roared Odin.

"You can cast off godhead for a while, put on the guise of a man and seek dire adventure, but all that while, inside your impersonation, you will know yourself to be Odin, who cannot die. So you shall never know the pleasure of true risk."

"Enough said!" cried Odin. "I hereby, for the space of this

adventure, cast off immortality and shrink myself into man-hood—thus!"

Odin stood before the massive gates, looking ludicrously small. His ermine robes had vanished with his divine stature and he was clad now in a blue cape. Tilted over his eye was a wide-brimmed black hat.

"Now, Loki," he said, "do you likewise."

Loki shrank himself down to the size of a man. They looked at each other and laughed uneasily.

"I feel so puny," said Odin. "So powerless. No use even taking my good spear, Gugnir. I wouldn't have the strength to lift it."

"True, my lord," said Loki. "But invincible weapons would deny you the pleasure of risk. We shall, of course, arm ourselves as befits our human condition."

"Suppose we are attacked by Giants or magic-wielding dwarfs. What good would our human weapons be then? Oh, I know, I know. The greater the risk, the greater the pleasure."

"On further consideration," said Loki, "I think we may allow ourselves a single weapon pulsing with the divine energy, but one of medium range. A hurling stone of Aesgard, perhaps. Such a stone well thrown should delay a Giant, say, giving us a chance to escape, and still allow a fine margin of risk."

"Get your stone, and let's go," said Odin.

5

Trapping Two Gods

Regnir was walking along the riverbank, thinking hard. "None of them will be easy to kill," he said to himself. "But Fafnir will be the hardest, so I'll leave him till last. He's always looking for fights, the bully, and the greater the odds the more he enjoys himself. Maybe if I wait long enough someone else will do the job for me."

He glimpsed his brother, Oter, who was spending this day as an enormous otter, lounging on a rock and picking the backbone out of a salmon. Regnir stared at him in loathing and walked on.

"That one won't be much easier," he thought. "They're all so damned big and strong, my family, and can transform themselves into things even bigger and stronger. While I am caged in this small, hideous body forever. My only power lies in my brains. I can outthink any one of those lard-heads, or all three of them put together. But I have to be very careful not to show what I'm thinking or they'll squash me like a bug. Oh well. I've deceived them so far, so I guess I can go on for a while longer.

Nevertheless, the time has come to start getting rid of them. But where shall I start?"

He heard someone coming and hid behind a tree. He saw two strangers walking toward him. One of them was very tall and broad-shouldered, and wore a full white beard. A wide-brimmed black hat was tilted over his eyes. Over his eye, rather. For now Regnir could see that he had only one eye; the other was covered by a patch. But that single eye was a dagger of light so piercing and blue that Regnir thought it must pass through the tree and reveal him hiding there.

The other man was smaller, graceful as a wildcat, had bushy orange hair and yellow eyes.

Regnir studied the strangers. He had no way of knowing that they were the gods Odin and Loki, who had shrunk themselves to human form. They did, indeed, look like mortal men, rather large ones, but they cast an inhuman brightness. And Regnir recognized that they were very important to him. He didn't know how or why, but felt that upon this hour his entire life was about to change. And feeling hardened into certainty as he heard the bearded one say:

"I'm getting hungry."

"Well, we're in a wood," said the other. "And our summer forests are full of game. And I hear a rushing of waters nearby. Do you fancy meat or fish?"

"Both," said the bearded man.

Regnir stepped out from behind his tree, and said: "Good day, sirs."

"Who are you?" snapped the orange-haired man. "And why were you hiding?"

"My name is Regnir, and I live nearby. I wasn't hiding; I was searching hollow trees for honeycombs."

"Honeycombs," murmured Odin. "Did you find any?"

"No, my lord. But if you're hungry I can guide you to a

stream where you can catch not only salmon but those who hunt them—bears and otters and such.''

"Guide away, little fellow," said Loki. "Why are you so ugly, incidentally? Are you a dwarf, perhaps? Or some kind of miniature ogre?''

Regnir heard someone coming and hid behind a tree.

"Something of both," said Regnir. "And less than either. Follow me if you will."

He led them to the riverbank and stood there pointing. "See?"

"See what?" said Loki.

"On that rock over there."

"Can that be a bear?" exclaimed Odin.

"An otter," said Regnir. "Outsize, but an otter."

"It's even big for a bear," whispered Loki to Odin. "Its hide will make a cape to draw the most beautiful Giantess from hearth and husband."

"Right now," growled Odin, "I'm more interested in otter steak."

"Steak first, pelt later," said Loki.

His hand flashed to his pouch. He pulled out the hurling stone and held it poised, calculating the distance to his target and the strength of the crosswind. Regnir watched in dismay. He knew that the huge otter's hide was so dense that it could hardly be pierced by arrow or spear. And its ogreish bones were strong and springy as iron barrel-hoops. Did this ridiculous man really expect to kill such a beast by throwing a stone?

Loki threw it now with an easy sidearm motion. "No force at all," thought Regnir sadly. "The stone will just tickle him." But the small round rock that Loki threw seemed to take on a life of its own when it left his hand.

Regnir heard the splat of it hitting Oter's head, heard his brother's skull cracking, saw the blood gush out of nostrils and mouth. The enormous shining otter fell dead, still clinging to the salmon he had caught and had not had time to eat.

"Fish and game both!" cried Loki. He turned to Regnir. "You're quite a guide, little fellow. Now let's see what kind of cook you are. Clean those creatures and roast them. And be very careful when you're skinning the otter. If you harm that magnificent pelt, I'll take your own hide off with my bare hands."

"No use to do all that out here with night drawing on," said Regnir. "Noble sirs, if you would but follow me, I'll lead you to my home. I have a superb flaying knife there, newly sharpened. And a proper roasting pit. Also a keg of mead and soft beds for you to sleep on."

"Good gnome," said Odin. "We accept your invitation."

"I'll run ahead to inform the servants," said Regnir. "Just follow me down this path about half a mile, and you'll come to my house."

"Do you live there alone?" asked Loki.

"No sir. My father lives there also. And my two—I mean my one brother. We do not often have the honor of entertaining such noble guests. You will find a warm welcome."

And he raced off. Odin and Loki followed, bearing the body of the otter between them.

Regnir ran as fast as he could and burst into the house. "Father, father!" he cried. "I bring bad news! Strangers have murdered Oter. They're coming now with his carcass and expect us to roast it for their dinner."

Hreidmar's bellow of fury rattled every bone in the house. "To work!" he roared. "To work! You, Regnir, prepare the keg and the cups. Cast sleepy herbs upon the fire. Rig the Hreidmar hammocks. You, Fafnir, put on your most fearsome form and await my signal."

The sons obeyed their father without hesitation. They knew that he was a master of such painful hospitality, and that they would profit from whatever he planned for his guests.

Odin and Loki had slung the body of the otter from a long pole which they balanced on their shoulders as they plodded through the woods, Loki in front. They came out of the forest into an open space and stood staring at the house of bone. Loki immediately recognized it for what it was and let his end of the pole slide to the ground.

"Quickly, my lord, let us flee!" he cried. "This is an ogre's den!"

"Flee? Me?" said Odin. "Not likely. I'm hungry and thirsty and mean to dine here, Ogres or not."

Just then they saw two skull cups floating toward them. A huge keg floated after the skulls. It was brimming with mead;

Each skull cup hovered within arm's reach of the men.

they could smell the honey and malt of it. Each skull hovered within arm's reach of the men. The keg tipped itself in the air and carefully poured mead into the skulls, not spilling a drop. Odin reached for his cup but it retreated slowly before him, floating toward the house. Odin followed, reaching for the skull that stayed just a bit beyond his reach. Loki had to follow. The skull stopped at the pelvis archway, allowing Odin to catch it. He emptied it in one long swallow.

Crying, "Regnir, we're here!" he strode through the archway, Loki following. They came into a huge chamber. A fire crackled in the hearth. "They're burning fatwood," Odin thought, for the fire cast a strong, sweet smell. Suddenly, he felt sleepy, as though he had already dined. He turned to look at Loki, and saw only a blur. He dropped into a large hammock that seemed to have slung itself from wall to bone wall.

Immediately, the hammock began to twirl, wrapping him in its folds. He tried to rip his way out but the slender ropes were like cable. He was caught. Netted like a fish. Helpless. He, who had been power itself, could not endure being helpless. Blackness took him.

He awoke to find himself chained to a rock outside the house. An iron ring had been sunk into the rock. Heavy iron chains passed through the ring and were bolted to iron collars about his neck, his waist, his wrists, and his ankles. Loki was beside him, chained in the same way. Planted in front of the rock were two legs, thick as tree trunks. Odin's gaze traveled up, up the whole length of the gigantic body to the ugliest face he had ever seen—something like a bearded warthog, complete with tusks. But the eyes were not animal eyes; they were dancing with malice.

His voice rumbled down at Odin. "I am Hreidmar, Lord Ogre of this domain. The carcass you have dropped in my yard was my son, Oter, who chose that form for his salmon fishing. Yes, you have murdered my best son, but I have two useful ones left. I can't introduce you to Regnir; he seems to have vanished for the moment. Grief-stricken, no doubt, by his brother's death. But Fafnir, my youngest, is eager to meet you."

As he spoke, an enormous weasel was gliding toward them; it was as big as a war-horse. Its eyes were pools of red fire; its mouth was bloody.

"In this form," said Hreidmar, "he can open you up and rummage among your entrails as a weasel does to a hare. My household, however, has a reputation for hospitality, even toward unwelcome guests. So I offer you an option."

He spoke to the weasel. "Be something else," he said.

Odin and Loki watched in horror as the weasel's skinny tail hooked itself, lost its hair, became a sting. Its body widened, grew hairy as a bee, sprouted antennae; it became, in fact, a giant scorpion.

"Contact with this one is more horrid, perhaps," said Hreidmar. "But the death it deals is less painful than what the weasel offers. For one touch of its sting will inject you with a paralyzing venom, and you will feel little pain as you watch yourself being devoured. You may choose between weasel and scorpion. Before you do that, though, consider a third option."

He snapped his fingers. The scorpion sprouted wings. Not the gauzy wings of an insect, or feathered bird wings, but ribbed leather ones. And its body changed as it rose—slimmed down, became long and sleek. Its face grew pointy. Its ears swiveled and tilted. Its feet wore talons, its narrow mouth was crowded with fangs. It had become a gigantic flying rat, bigger than an eagle.

"Fafnir's third incarnation," said Hreidmar. "A vampire bat. Should you choose his attentions he will dive upon you, sink his fangs into your throat and drink your rich blood. A colorful death, less messy for us in a way, allows us to strip the bloodless flesh away and begin drying the bones for construction. But, as

I promised, I shan't consult my own convenience, but give you the chance to choose. So choose, strangers. Choose your death—weasel, scorpion, or bat. Which is it to be? Don't ponder too long, or I shall have to choose for you."

Regnir had been hiding, melting into a shadow as only Gnomes can do, listening to his father's threatening, and watching Fafnir change shape. Now, he knew, he had to act. While he wanted the captives to be thoroughly frightened, he didn't want them killed—not yet. For he smelled wealth upon them.

Swiftly, he began to dig. He drove his spade-shaped hands into the earth, scooping out great clumps until a hole yawned at his feet. He dived into the hole, and crouching on stumpy, twisted legs began to tunnel toward the rock where Odin and Loki were chained. He dug his way to a spot directly under Loki. He heard his father's voice.

"You won't choose? Very well, I shall choose for you."

Loki, frozen by fear, heard another voice speak out of the ground. "Offer blood ransom! Quickly!"

"Blood ransom!" croaked Loki to Hreidmar.

"Blood ransom, yes," rumbled Hreidmar. "Your blood for my son's."

Odin's voice rang out fresh and clear. "*Weir gelt* he means, good Ogre. Gold in payment for your son's life, much gold."

"How much is much?" growled Hreidmar.

"You name it."

"Enough to cover my son's hide, every hair of it."

"But that hide is as big as a tent," said Odin. "I don't know if I have enough to cover it."

"Then what you have will be going to your heirs," said Hreidmar. "And I mean immediately."

"Well, perhaps I can scrape up enough. Unchain us and we'll go fetch it."

"Do you take me for a fool?" roared Hreidmar. "You'll be

unchained when I see the color of your gold, not before."

"But how can we get it for you unless you let us go?"

"That's your problem," said the ogre. "And you'd better solve it quickly. I'm growing impatient and the bat is very thirsty."

Again the underground voice spoke: "One must stay, the other go. Tell him, tell him!"

"Wait, Sir Ogre," groaned Loki. "There's a way to do it. Let one of us go to fetch the gold and hold the other until he returns."

"Very well," rumbled Hreidmar. "I'll keep the old one. He seems more important."

"Where is it?" whispered Loki to Odin.

Ordinarily, Loki would have been the last one Odin would have trusted with the secret of his hoard. But now, he knew, there was no other way out.

"It's far to the south," he whispered. "In a cave under the river Rhine, where it makes its fourth bend. Here, take my ring so that those who guard the trove will know you come from me and let you into the cave."

Now Loki had long lusted for this ring of Odin's. Of all the jewels that adorned the Gods and Goddesses of Aesgard, this one was the most magnificent. So cunningly wrought was it, of gold so pure, it seemed that some magical smith had caught a handful of sunlight and twisted it into the shape of a ring. And through his pain and fear Loki felt a glimmer of pure greed and told himself, "No matter what, I shall have this ring for my own, and never let it go."

As soon as he saw Loki being unshackled, Regnir climbed out of his tunnel and hurried to the river. One of the secret skills he had taught himself was to speak bird language. He whistled up to a gull now, and said:

"See that orange-pated fellow heading south? Follow him

for me; see where he goes. Then return with all speed and tell me. You owe me a favor for getting rid of Oter. Now you gulls can feast on the shoals of salmon he would have devoured."

"I am honored to do your bidding, O Regnir," said the gull, and soared away. The gnome ran back to his tunnel and took up his post near Odin.

Hreidmar kept Odin chained to the rock as they waited for Loki to return with the gold. Nor did he offer his captive food or drink, meaning to make him suffer until he was actually ransomed. But Regnir, who still lurked underground, popped out of his hole that first night, bringing Odin roasted ground-squirrel and a flagon of springwater.

At first Odin would not accept the offering, but glared at Regnir out of his one eye. "You misshapen little fiend," he grated. "First you betrayed us into killing your brother, then delivered us into the hands of your monster kin. I'll accept no favors from you."

"As you will," said Regnir. "But my father means to torment you with hunger and thirst until your friend returns with the gold—and that, as you know, may take a long time."

"So be it," said Odin. "Begone!"

"I do you no favor," said Regnir, "but offer something for a price. Say nothing to my father about my part in Oter's death, and I'll keep you fed for as long as you are chained to this rock."

Odin was about to refuse again but the savor of the roasted squirrels overpowered him. He was just too hungry to keep any resolutions. He snatched the spitted carcasses from Regnir and gobbled them up. Upended the flagon and gulped the water.

"More," he grunted.

"But do you agree to my terms?"

"By the fire and ice of deepest Hel, I do. Kill off the rest of your charming family, for all I care. In fact, the death of your ogre father and monster brother would leave the world much improved—especially if you slit your own throat afterward."

"But do you agree to my terms?" insisted Regnir. "Will you keep silent about how I led you to Oter?"

"I agree, I agree; I've already told you so. Now get busy and roast me more squirrels. Or a partridge, perhaps, or a fat hare. Something with a bit more meat to it."

While Loki was gone, Regnir kept to his burrow, coming out only at night with food for Odin. All this time, however, he was listening for the screech which would mean that his gull had returned. He waited and waited, wondering whether Loki had simply fled to save his own life, leaving his companion to be murdered. And Odin, chained to his rock, was trying not to think the same thought.

On the sixth night, though, shortly before dawn, Regnir did hear a gull cry, and popped out of his hole. It was a moonless night, very dark, but a thicker darkness dropped, and Regnir felt a weight on his shoulder.

"I am weary, weary," gasped the gull. "I followed him south for three days and nights—to the fourth bend of a river called the Rhine—saw what he did there, then sped back faster than I had gone."

"Gold! Gold!" cried Regnir. "Did he find gold there?"

"He took it from under the river, from a cave dug into the bank. Oh, good gnome, that cave holds a wondrous hoard of gold. He sewed two mainsails into sacks and filled them full, and the heap of gold in the cave seemed unshrunken."

"Did you mark the spot? Can you find it again?"

"I can take you to it any time you want," said the gull. "But will you do a watery magic and send fish my way? For I am weary with traveling and very, very hungry."

"You shall feast!" cried Regnir. "I'll send you shoals of salmon, honest gull. Fine sleek males, females bursting with roe! Fly away now and start fishing! I'll call upon you again when I want to go south."

6

Ransom and Curse

Loki returned to the bone house leading a gigantic ox. Slung over its back were fat sacks that clinked with every swaying step the beast took.

"Hoo hah!" roared Hreidmar. "Make ready for the ransom! Fafnir . . . Regnir . . . take hold of your brother's pelt and spread it upon the grass!"

They sprang to obey and the three ogres walked slowly over the meadow, laying the pelt. As they went, they sang a Rune of Increase:

Corn-mother, Norn-mother,
you who arrange and disarrange,
and play with change,
making big the small
and small the big,
enlarging raindrop to sea
and seed to tree,
calf to cow
and piglet to pig—
reducing the bright and strong
to rust and dust,
making death
rhyme with breath . . .
Corn-mother, Norn-mother,
help us now . . .
Stretch this hide
to a bowshot long
and a bowshot wide . . .

And as Hreidmar and his sons passed over the grass they felt their prayer being answered—felt the pelt stretching in their hands. It stretched and stretched. For it must be understood that an ogre's bow is the trunk of an ash tree split in half. This bow when pulled to the full reach of an ogre's arms will send an arrow with such force that it will go through a stone wall a quarter of a mile away and kill whatever is hiding behind that wall. So . . . the otter's pelt now covered the entire meadow.

Loki, seeing the hide stretch like that, knew he didn't have enough gold to cover it and that he would have to try a magic of his own. So he swiftly did a sun trick. He multiplied dazzles, making each gold piece cast a triple gleam, coining sequins of blinding golden light that confused the sight and seemed like gold itself.

Hreidmar strode across the meadow and loomed over Loki and his ox. He looked down at them, grinning. "Unload your beast," he said.

"I can't lift the bags," said Loki. "They're much too heavy. Perhaps you're strong enough."

Hreidmar reached down, grasped the heavy ropes that lashed the sacks and broke them as easily as if they were thread, and took hold of a sack. But he couldn't lift it off the ox's back; it was too heavy for him.

"Fafnir!" he called.

Fafnir came to them and lifted one sack in each hand. He staggered slightly but walked off with them. When he reached the pelt he ripped open one of the sacks and upended it. Regnir gasped as he saw the gold spilling onto the hide.

"Spread it evenly," called Loki. "No double layers."

"Remember," said Hreidmar, "every hair must be covered. Or you and your friend forfeit your lives."

"Every hair shall be covered," said Loki.

Indeed, when Fafnir had emptied one sack, opened the other and emptied it also, the enormous pelt was tiled with gold. But Regnir, watching greedily, saw one hair of the otter's muzzle bristling in a chink of gold, a single hair under the shadow of its nose.

"Not enough!" he cried. "One hair is still uncovered by gold. See here?" And he pointed to the muzzle.

"I have no more gold," said Loki.

"Too bad," said Hreidmar. "Fafnir, my son, you may kill them now."

"Wait!" called Regnir. He darted to Loki and seized his hand. "You have this ring—three loops of purest gold curiously twined. It will buy your lives."

"It's not mine to give," said Loki. "It belongs to him." He pointed to Odin.

"Let them have it," said Odin. He didn't raise his voice but it seemed to fill the meadow.

Loki felt the blood draining from his heart as he allowed Regnir to twist the ring off his finger. But he did not dare refuse.

Regnir ran to his father, holding out the ring. "Here, sire. It's a kingly gem. It will look well on your finger."

"Unchain me," said Odin. Regnir went to the rock and unbolted the shackles.

Odin shook himself, flexed his arms and legs, and put on his wide-brimmed black hat. He stared at Hreidmar out of his one eye. And the ogre, who had never known fear, felt that eye go through him like a dagger made of blue light.

"That ring is your doom," said Odin. "Each loop a circlet of bane for whoever wears it except me. So you are triply cursed, mine host. But will die a singular death."

Hreidmar roared with fury and charged toward Odin. At this point, however, Odin decided that his first experiment with mortality was honorably concluded. With a wave of his hand, then, he resumed his godhead and vanished, taking Loki with him.

On their way back to Aesgard, Odin said: "Loki, I want you to manage the curse."

"How do you mean, sire?"

"See that it destroys them all—the whole fiendish tribe. When the ring has done its work, cleanse it of evil enchantment and return it to me."

"As you will, my lord."

7

Death with Father

fter the gods had departed, Regnir felt himself bursting with a wild, joyous greed. So far his plan was working perfectly; now he was ready for the biggest step of all. He watched his father crouching over the pelt, scooping up great handfuls of gold and letting them sift though his fingers. Regnir turned to his brother. "Let's go into the woods," he said. "I have something to talk to you about."

"Why can't we talk here?" said Fafnir.

"I don't want *him* to overhear," whispered Regnir.

The sons of Hreidmar walked off into the forest. "Brother," said Regnir, "which of your transformations is the most terrible—weasel, scorpion, or vampire bat?"

"Bat, I suppose," said Fafnir. "I can rend and tear, munch and crunch in any of these forms. But things with wings seem to frighten folk the most. Sometimes, when the moon is bright, the very shadow of my wings will scare someone so badly that he will fall dead before I can sink my fangs into him. A disadvantage in a way, because I prefer to drink blood out of a living throat."

"Well," said Regnir, "suppose I were to tell you that there

is a creature more frightful than any vampire bat—bigger, stronger, scarier, more deadly in every way. A creature whom even Giants fear and the Gods avoid."

"I knew there was something somewhere," cried Fafnir. "I knew it! I knew it! And someday I'll be it!"

"Will you? It's not easy to be."

"I will, I will! But what is it exactly? Do you know?"

"I'll describe it for you. In shape it's like a lizard, but a gigantic one, bigger than our barn. Its hide is made of sliding leather scales, hard as iron; no weapon can pierce it. It has a ridged spine, a spiked tail that can flail down a phalanx of men, squashing them like beetles in their armor. Great ribbed wings it has, and claws that are huge hooks. A maw full of dagger teeth, and, worst of all, or rather best of all—"

"Yes, yes—what?"

"It spits fire," said Regnir. "One gust of its flaming breath can incinerate a troop, or a fleet, or burn down a stand of trees."

"Oh glory," shouted Fafnir. "Gory, gory glory!"

"Its name is Dragon," said Regnir.

"Oh wise little brother," cried Fafnir, catching up Regnir and hugging him tight, "you have given name and shape to my dearest dream! Does your wisdom go further? Can you tell me how to achieve dragonhood?"

"Let me down," said Regnir. "You're breaking my ribs. . . . Thank you. Now, let us reason it out together. The dragon is of all monsters the most monstrous. To be worthy of such incarnation you must be prepared to do the most monstrous of deeds."

"Murder? But I've killed and killed."

"Only enemies, though, or those unlucky enough to have something you want. That doesn't take a monster. Ordinary warriors do that all the time. No, my dear Fafnir. What we must consider for you now is murder most foul. A primal abomination."

"Well, what? Tell me, tell me . . ."

"Patricide."

"What's that exactly?"

"Killing one's father."

"Hreidmar?"

"In your case, yes. He's the only father you have."

"But that doesn't seem so special. I've had it in mind for a long time."

"You haven't done it, though."

"Well, no . . ."

"What are you waiting for?"

"If I kill him, I'll become a dragon? Is that what you say?"

"That's what I promise."

"Big as that barn? With ribbed wings and a spiked tail and such claws and teeth, and all that?"

"The whole works, brother. Go get him. You'll find him where we left him, counting the gold. Which will be all ours, incidentally."

"Come then," said Fafnir. "I need you as a witness in case anyone questions my right to become a dragon."

"How will you attend to him—as weasel, scorpion, or bat?"

"As myself, I think. I'll enjoy it more."

Fafnir leaned over and uprooted a tree. Snapped off its branches and swung it about his head a few times.

"Nice balance," he said. "I'll just bash in his head with this."

"Call him away from the pelt first," said Regnir. "No use getting blood all over that beautiful gold."

8

Asking the Ring

Regnir was playing with Odin's ring. He had slid it off the finger of his dead father, and, to his delight, it had immediately shrunk, becoming small enough for him to wear. Its twined loops smouldered on his finger, sending a soft fire through his body. Something told him to turn the ring to the right. He did so. A nest came spinning out of a tree, spun in the air above his head and began to tip, gently spilling eggs into his hand. Blue jay eggs, by their size. He chortled with glee, and one by one cracked them open and sucked out the rich slime. He loved birds' eggs and had always climbed trees and robbed nests.

This nest spun away, and Regnir turned the ring to the left. Muffled voices arose from under his feet, a chorus of them. He couldn't make out what they were saying. He scooped out a hole and plastered his ear against it.

"Master, master," he heard. "You have summoned us. Now tell us what to do."

"Who are you?"

"The Delving Dwarfs. How can we serve you?"

"I'll let you know," he whispered, and covered up the hole.

Flaming with joy, he twisted the ring again and again. Took it off and spun it on his palm. But nothing happened. "It holds mighty secrets," he said to himself. "But I'll practice and practice and unlock its powers. It bears a curse, the one-eyed stranger said. Yessss—a curse for my enemies. For myself, I'll turn the bane into a blessing, and gain mastery over all."

He hurried to the riverbank where he had told his brother to meet him. He stopped short, shocked by what he saw. Fafnir was changing himself into a dragon, but slowly, gazing into the mirroring surface of the river, watching himself change. So far, he had done only his head. A scaly, stone-eyed dragon's head sat on his broad ogre shoulders. The rest of him was unchanged. And he was amusing himself by spitting little spurts of flame, roasting frogs as they roosted on the lily pads.

"Finish changing yourself," said Regnir. "Then go under. Robbers will be coming soon."

"You'd better drop that tone," growled Fafnir. "Dragons are not ordered to do things; they're humbly requested." He spat a gout of fire at Regnir's hairy toes, making him hop in terror.

"Your pardon, O Dragon," cried Regnir. "I humbly request you to complete your transformation and enter the river so that you may guard our treasure."

"That's better," said Fafnir, and finished changing himself. Now a great green and gold dragon crouched on the riverbank, staring out of stone eyes at the twisted dwarf.

"Thank you," said Regnir. "And remember this: Don't blow fire while underwater . . . or you'll make the river boil and be thoroughly cooked before you can surface."

"When can I expect some action?" grunted Fafnir.

"The word of our treasure has undoubtedly spread, and will be attracting every thief in this part of the country—which means almost everyone. So they should provide you with plenty of sport—and food."

"Does that mean I'll have to stay down there? I'll mildew."

"It won't be for very long," said Regnir. "I promise. As soon as I steal the larger hoard, now buried in the Rhine, I'll have it brought here and hide it in one of the Black Mountain caves.

"When can I expect some action?" grunted Fafnir.

We'll move this gold up there also, and you'll be able to guard
it all while enjoying the mountain air."

"How long are you talking about, though? When are you
going to the Rhine?"

"Soon . . . soon . . . as soon as I master all the tricks of
this ring, which, among other things, seems to give me dominion
over the Delving Dwarfs. I'll need a legion of them to carry the
Rhinegold from the river bottom to the mountain top."

"That ring," said Fafnir. "Don't forget it's half mine. I mean
to wear it when I resume my own form."

"Of course, of course," said Regnir. "We are equal partners,
dear brother. In all that we have stolen and shall steal we share
and share alike. Farewell now. I'm going to work with the ring
a bit. Please go under now. Thieves should be diving in very
soon, perhaps in time for your lunch."

Regnir scurried off. "Partners, indeed," he snarled to himself. "As soon as I get rid of him it will all be mine, mine, mine!
But not yet, not yet. I need him alive a while to guard this gold
until I go after the other. Not yet . . . soon, but not yet . . ."

9

Blue-blade

Odin made it a point to watch important battles and to reward those who did especially brave deeds. To some he gave swift horses; others received sleek ships to go a-viking in. Genuine heroes were given weapons out of the magical Aesgard armory.

To a favorite of his, a warrior named Sigmund of the princely Valsung blood, he gave his own dagger. And, although Sigmund was very tall for a mortal, the god's dagger made him a superbly long sword. Its blade was of blue meteor-iron, dug out of a veined rock that had fallen from the stars. Forged by Smith Dwarfs, its cutting edge was so sharp that it could shear through helmet or breastplate like a kitchen knife through cheese. To Sigmund this sword was alive, part of his body, an extension of his own arm. He gave it a name, Blue-blade. And Blue-blade, wielded by Sigmund, made a circle of whirling death, scything down his enemies like stalks of ripe wheat.

But those gifted by the Gods are often envied by mortals, and so ownership of the wondrous sword was to threaten Sigmund's life. Indeed, his castle was attacked by the troops of a treacherous cousin who had come as an honored guest and had quartered his men in the courtyard. These men had kept their weapons while pretending to go to sleep. They arose in the darkest hour, slaughtered Sigmund's men and stormed into the castle.

Sigmund fought desperately. His sword was a circle of blue fire in the torchlight. He cut down twenty attackers, cut his way to the courtyard. Bleeding from a score of wounds, he leaped on his horse and galloped away, bearing his pregnant wife with him.

His cousin, maddened by the thought that he was losing the sword he wanted so much, burned the castle to the ground, and set off in pursuit of Sigmund. With fifty horsemen he raced after the Valsung prince, following a trail of blood. But they lost the trail when they came to a thick forest.

Sigmund led his wife deep into the woods until he could go no farther. "My strength is gone," he said. "They have killed me. Now go hide yourself, my darling."

She clutched at him. "I won't leave you."

"You must . . . for the sake of the child you carry. They will try to kill it too, especially if it's a boy who might grow up to avenge his father."

She hung about his neck, moaning. Gently, he unwound her arms. He raised his sword and spoke to it. "You are Odin's gift; you must not fall into base hands." Then with his last strength he snapped the blade in half.

When his wife saw him do that, she burst into wild sobs. He embraced her again, kissed her wet face, and sank to the ground. "Tell my son about his father," he whispered. And died.

She was a princess of an ancient warrior clan. She had been trained to cope. She bit back her sobs and tried to think clearly. She had to burn the body, or bury it, or it would be eaten. Aye, they would come—fox and crow, wood rat, and the tunneling worm; they would feast upon that beloved flesh. Burning was best, cleanest, and most honorable. But the child was making itself felt within her. She knew she didn't have time to find dry wood and build a funeral pyre. She snatched up the broken sword blade and began to dig. Then she felt her pains begin and knew she would not have time to make a grave. She stooped, kissed his eyes, scraped some leaves over him—rushed to a tall birch and, hardly knowing what she was doing, stabbed the blade into the ground under the tree until it was hidden. Then went deeper into the woods to bear her child.

10

Gnome and Nymph

umping along southward toward the Rhine, Regnir became more and more fearful of what he might find there. "By the nature of things, I must run into trouble," he muttered to himself. "If a dread dragon watches over my treasure, this larger Rhine hoard may be guarded by something even more fearsome. What could that be? What's more fearsome than a dragon, except a bigger one? And whatever it is, will I be able to witch it away with this ring? I doubt it, somehow. For the ring was part of the treasure, and by some sympathetic magic may be drawing me to my doom. Perhaps that is the very curse put upon the ring— 'Whoever wears it will be drawn southward in an honest effort to steal the Rhinegold and there be devoured by some monster'. . . . Is that it?—Why am I thinking like this? I'll frighten myself right out of my shoon. But cowardice, after all, is what's kept me alive in my ogreish family, runt that I am. Yes . . . sheer funk plus greed plus very sharp wits—a matchless recipe for survival. Before I enter the Rhine I must carefully plan what to do in case I meet a monster."

Just then he heard a mewing sound. He looked about. The trees cast a dappled shade, patches of brightness and sliding shadows; it was hard to see. His foot hit something that clanked. Leaping away, he saw that he had kicked a skeleton in armor. The bones of a very tall man lay among leaves and pinecones. The wide chest bones wore a breastplate; the skull wore a helmet. Regnir cast about for a sword, thinking that its hilt might be jeweled. But the sword was gone. He found something else though—the bones of a woman. He looked closely, but could find no rings or anklets.

"A warrior," he thought. "Must have been wounded in battle and dragged himself into these woods and bled to death, no doubt. And this is his wife who died with him, or shortly thereafter."

Regnir was about to go on his way when he heard the same mewing sound. It seemed to be coming out of a deep shadow under an oak tree. He went closer and to his amazement saw a baby shining there. Sunlight lanced through the leaves and gilded the child's hair. It was a pale floss. And his eyes were so blue they looked almost purple. He shone like a star.

"Why haven't the animals eaten it?" thought Regnir. "It's so plump and fine."

Then he saw the mark of an animal's body on the ground next to the babe—a large animal. And he realized what must have happened. Beasts had suckled the babe—a wolf, perhaps, or a she-bear.

"Mysteries . . . enchantments," mumbled Regnir to himself. "It's being protected by the Gods. I'll leave it right here."

He started away again. But his footsteps dragged. He found himself turning and going back to where the babe lay. "Plump and fine," he said to himself. "Yes. And very tasty, no doubt, for those who fancy babies. Ugh! . . . but a delicious tidbit to fling to a monster who might be pursuing me. It will stop and feast and give me a chance to escape. Yes . . ."

Moving swiftly, he tore vines from the tree and began to weave them into a basket. His fingers flew. He finished the basket,

*Sunlight lanced through the leaves
and gilded the child's hair. . . .
He shone like a star.*

lincd it with grass, put the baby in, slung it over his shoulder and humped away.

"Heavy," he muttered. "And I'll have to carry it a long way—and feed it now and then. Very pesky. But it may divert whatever monster lurks in the Rhine and give me a chance to take the treasure."

Regnir came to the Rhine, finally. He hid the basket among reeds and stood on the shore, gazing at the bend of river. A Rhine-maiden saw something move on the bank. She flashed through the water, reached a long arm, plucked Regnir off the bank, then swam to a rock to see what she had caught. Laughing, she stood him on her lap, clutching him tightly, and examined him from head to foot.

He heard her gurgling with laughter. "Hairy ears, hairy toes," he heard her say. "All smooth on top, but the rest of it's as furry as a bear cub. Not as cute and cuddly, though."

"Let me see," called another sister who sat on another rock. "Catch!"

And the first one tossed him to her sister, who caught him by one ankle and held him upside down as she poked his belly and pinched his hams. "Pudgy little thing," she said. "Quite ugly. What can it be?"

"Ask it," called the third sister. "It looks rather clever. Perhaps it can speak."

"Indeed I can speak, and do more than that," cried Regnir.

"Really? What?"

"All kinds of magic," said Regnir. "I'm a very powerful wizard. I can reward my friends and harm my enemies. So be advised, ladies. Do not tweak my ears or toes—or poke my belly or twist my nose, or pinch other parts of me. For those sort of things make me very angry. And I am terrible when aroused."

He felt the nymph gasping with laughter as she clutched him to her. Heard them all laughing. Silver peals of Rhine-maiden laughter dinned about him.

"What you are, dear wizard, is a thief," she gasped. "For you wear the ring that was worn by that other one who came here not long ago—that orange-haired clown. So you must have stolen it from him. And have come here now to steal more of the gold, right?"

"Wrong," growled Regnir. "Let me go or you'll regret it."

"No, Pudge. You'll do the regretting. Before we're through with you you'll wish you had never laid eyes on us."

The other sisters had climbed onto the rock in the meantime, and the three of them sat there, passing him from one to the other—not really hurting him, but teasing roughly, tweaking ears and nose, and plucking hairs out of his toes.

"Well, what shall we do with this little thief?" asked the first sister.

"Let's keep him," said the second sister. "He can be useful. He can comb our hair with a silver comb, and clip our toenails, and polish the gold. Yes . . . and gather blackberries and honeycombs and succulent cresses for our meals."

"He looks sullen," said the third sister. "Perhaps he'll be more trouble than he's worth."

"Perhaps," said the second one. "But let's try. He'll need lots of training and it'll be lots of fun. We'll whip him soundly twice a day and perhaps a few times in between."

"He'll try to escape."

"How can he? We'll keep him leashed. And even if he should make it to shore, what then? Our legs are so much longer—we can catch him in two strides."

To his horror, Regnir felt himself growing sleepy. He was being tamed, he knew, by too much handling. He was falling under their spell. He knew he had to think very hard or he would find himself enslaved forever. But it was difficult to think. Their bodies were so long and richly moulded, and bursting with such health. They cast a wild caramel scent of sun and water. As the nymph held him squirming on her long thigh he felt himself sinking like a seed into rich, mothering earth.

Mothering—yes! What was left of his wits leaped hungrily at the thought. Oh yes . . .

"Gracious maidens," he said, "you guard a treasure. But I bring you something you will value even more."

"What? Where? What are you babbling about?"

"It's there, there where I was standing. In a little basket hidden in the reeds."

The second sister dived off the rock and swam toward shore. The one holding Regnir clutched him tighter. He felt her strong fingers digging into him, felt the sleek, cabled muscles of her thigh under him, felt his will dissolving.

The swimmer clambered onshore and searched among the reeds. She plucked out the basket and screamed with joy. The one holding Regnir slid him off her lap and dived into the water,

"Gracious maidens," Regnir said, "you guard a treasure.
But I bring you something
you will value even more."

followed by the third sister. And Regnir gloated as he saw them lift the shining babe out of its basket. They had forgotten their captive. In the raging fever of their untried motherhood they forgot the gold they were supposed to be guarding. They were snatching the babe from one another, nuzzling every inch of it, laughing and sobbing, trying to give it their breasts, chewing berries and trying to kiss the pulp into its mouth as if it were a fledgling bird.

And Regnir was able to slip into the water and search until

he found the treasure cave. Was able to summon the Delving Dwarfs, who dug their way up into the river bottom from beneath. Upon Regnir's command, they began to cart off the gold.

Regnir watched them, drooling, crying, "Faster! Faster!" He punched and kicked them, although they were working as fast as they could. They had taken about half the hoard when Regnir heard the laughter of the nymphs coming closer.

"Be off!" he shouted to the dwarfs. "Vanish!"

They burrowed into the river bottom like sand crabs, and disappeared. Regnir swam away, snarling with glee. "Only half," he muttered to himself. "But that half added to what I have makes me the richest creature in the entire world, no doubt. And I'll be coming back one day for the other half. Aieee! Aieee! How I admire meeee . . ."

11

Loki Looks Ahead

Time is not the same in Aesgard as in Midgard. The Gods simply cannot be measured on a human scale. A year for mortals is a short winter's afternoon for the Gods. This is why impatience is viewed in various heavens as not merely a childish habit, but a sin.

And now seventeen years had passed before Odin thought again about those who had tricked him and chained him and stolen his ring. He summoned Loki to his throne room and glared down at him. Loki felt his master's voice falling from a great height, crushing him to the ground. The throne was made of crystal; Odin's beard seemed spun of snow. They borrowed light from each other and cast such a brightness that Loki could not bear to raise his eyes.

"Well," boomed Odin. "What do you have to say?"

"Are you talking about the curse of the ring, my lord?"

"That's exactly what I'm talking about."

"I have not been negligent, I swear. I've just been letting things ripen."

"They should be rotten ripe by now," said Odin. "I expect faster action when I ask that something be done. Tell me exactly how things stand."

"O Master, my devotion to you is so great that I have been delving into things you have perhaps forgotten, trying to fuse events, old and new, into a happening that will not only satisfy but delight you."

"Words, words, words!" roared Odin. "Stop praising your intentions and tell me plainly what goes on down there."

"First of all, my lord, the Ogre-in-chief, Hreidmar, the one who chained you to a rock and threatened you with such horrors, has already been punished. Not long after we left, his son Fafnir uprooted a tree and pounded his head to a pulp."

"This Fafnir—does he still live?"

"Yes."

"Still terrorizing folk as weasel, scorpion, and vampire bat?"

"He has promoted himself to dragon now and spends most of his time in that form."

"How about that little scurvy one—what was his name? Regnir? The one who led us into the whole mess. Is he still alive too?"

"For the moment. But the brothers are feuding now."

"Over the treasure they stole—my treasure?"

"That gold, sire, is the chief element of the curse; even though it is out of your possession, it still works your will."

"What do you mean? Stop talking in riddles."

"The curse that you uttered and stamped with your awful authority, the curse of the ring, works like a legion of clever, invisible needlewomen, sewing deeds and hopes and dreams and crimes into a vast tapestry. Works somewhat as the Norns do, actually—but all within the scope of your own purpose.

"For Regnir, who is the cleverest brother, had the treasure shifted to a mountain cave, and persuaded his brother, the dragon, to guard it. What he could not foretell, for all his cleverness, was that he would find his own way barred. Yes, the dragon now crouches before the cave, claiming the entire hoard for himself, and threatening anyone who approaches the cave, especially if that one is Regnir. And the gnome, burning with greed, half-crazed by rage, is planning how to kill the dragon."

"Sounds interesting," said Odin. "How is he going to go about it?"

"Oh, I shall send him a few ideas. Remember the Valsung prince named Sigmund, to whom you gave your blue dagger to use as a sword—and who, in fact, used it so heroically that his deeds have become a song? Remember Sigmund?"

"I do. He was a real hero. He provided me with many a fine spectacle. They don't make them like him anymore."

"One more was made, my lord, just like him. Sigmund was treacherously killed, as you know. And his wife survived by only a few days."

"Yes . . ."

"Well, his wife gave birth to a child before she died. A son. And the babe was found and adopted by those who raised him amid healthy ordeal—so that now, at the age of seventeen, he is strong and brave, a true son of his father."

"What is his name?"

"He is called Siegfried. I mean him to fight the dragon."

"And how can this untried youth, for all his noble heritage, possibly prevail against so dreadful a monster as Fafnir?"

"Long odds, my master, long, long odds. But is not such uncertainty the very essence of conflict, and the true test of courage? Think how interesting it will be to watch this almost hopeless battle. Think how your heart will rejoice if, indeed, Siegfried vanquishes the dragon. And, if he does not, well, there is always another day, another way. Nor will one defeat diminish the power of the ring, or abate the curse."

"Well," said Odin. "You sound like you know what you're doing, after all. Proceed with your arrangements."

Whereupon he dismissed Loki from the throne room, and the matter from his mind.

12

Runes Are Magic Songs

Regnir bent his vast cunning toward finding a way to get rid of Fafnir without risk to himself. Feverishly, he wove plots and shuffled ploys. But every one of his plans collided with a stubborn fact— Fafnir's monstrous power. He had been dangerous enough in his own gigantic ogre form, and even larger and more deadly as weasel, scorpion, and vampire bat. But the new reality of him as an enormous armored flail-tailed, razor-clawed, fire-spitting dragon turned any idea of opposing him into a nightmare.

Regnir was pacing the meadow near the bone house, thinking of these things and growing more desperate with each thought.

"What can I do?" he groaned. "He's calmly appropriating the entire hoard. How can I bear it?"

Suddenly, he heard a thin voice. He looked about, saw nothing. Again he heard a little voice. It seemed to be coming from his own hand. Could it be the ring? He raised his hand to his face, listening, staring.

Loki, hovering invisibly, instructed the ring, which began

to chirp at Regnir. "Louder!" he cried, pressing it to his hairy ear. "Speak louder!"

"Ask me what you would know, master, and I shall answer."

Music is the shortest road to enchantment. And, when questioning the future, Regnir knew, it is necessary to speak in rhyme, which is spoken music. Looking down into the twined loops of the ring, he chanted:

Tell me, please,
who can slay my brother
and restore my gold—
ogre, giant, or warrior bold?

He heard the ring chirp:

None of these
but another—
an orphan brave
with blade of blue
alone can do
what you crave.

Regnir chortled and danced. "Thank you, ring, thank you. But where do I find this orphan?"

"Remember the babe you gave to the Rhine maidens? Go back to where you found him; you will find him there again. Offer him to the Sooty Ones as an apprentice smith. The lad will forge a wondrous sword and fight your battle for you."

"Thank you, thank you."

"Aye," said Loki to himself as he flew away. "I have obeyed my lord, instructed the ring, and launched the curse against Regnir and Fafnir. But Odin, when he reclaims the ring, may find that a curse is more easily uttered than withdrawn. Ah, these are dark matters. . . . Shall I consult the Norn? A single misstep now will place me in utmost peril. High God or Fatal Hag—both offer friendship. Hoh hah! Such favor is more dangerous than enmity. So weiroo and whirlaway! I'll do as I choose and lie about everything . . ."

Down below, Regnir was wasting no time. He was on his way to the glade where he had stumbled on the skeletons and found the shining babe, and he was humping along as fast as he could.

The names of the Rhine-maidens were Arla, Dure, and Helge, and they had given Siegfried a very happy childhood. They were like lionesses in their mothering, full of body warmth, but strict in teaching him lessons of survival. They taught him to breathe underwater, to slow his heartbeat so that he could live under the frozen river when winter came. He could swim like a pike, dive like a cormorant, run like a stag.

The child grew into a boy, the boy into a youth of shocking beauty. Hair and skin were all one color, coppery gold. His eyes were a deep violet, almost purple. He looked, in fact, as though he were a brother of the Rhine-maidens. And since their appearance never changed, they all seemed the same age when he reached seventeen.

But he was growing out of his own sense of himself. The hours passed in a daze. Dreams were no longer a throng of colored pictures, but teasing puzzles. One night he dreamed that he was running through the forest and the sisters were chasing him, calling, "Hei hoe, hei hoe," as though they were hunting. They chased him through thickets of sleep, and when he awoke, the dream followed him. As he sat on a sun-warmed rock, munching a honeycomb, Helge came to him and began to kiss the stickiness off his face.

He pushed her into the river. She caught his ankle as she

The child grew into a boy, the boy into a youth of shocking beauty.
Hair and skin were
all one color, coppery gold.

fell and pulled him in too. When he climbed onto the rock again,
all three of them were waiting for him.

    "The time has come," said Arla. "You must marry."

    "Whom?"

    "Us, of course."

"All three?"

"Or just one, if you prefer."

"Which one?"

"Whichever you choose."

"What will the others do?"

"Who knows," said Helge. "Be jealous, I suppose."

"I can't choose," said Siegfried.

"You must," said Dure.

"No. I'll marry you all."

"All at once, or one after the other?"

"You decide."

"We'll let you know," said Arla. They dived off the rock and swam away.

That night he dreamed of a birch tree and heard something chime:

I am your father's blade
buried in this glade.
Under the singing tree
you will uncover me.
I am only a shard
but fire me hot
and hammer me hard
and restore
me to myself
once more
the sword
your father bore.

He awoke in the first flush of dawn, knowing that he was not ready to be a bridegroom. He slipped into the water and swam without a ripple, so silently that the sisters did not awake. He reached the bank and vanished into the woods.

*Among all the trees clad in summer leaves
stood a bare white birch sheathed in ice.*

He traveled night and day, not knowing where he was going but guided by some sure sense beyond his knowledge, like a migrating bird. Finally, he reached a clearing in the forest where trees cast a dappled shade, patches of brightness, sliding shadows. Something told him he was where he was meant to be. He stood still as a deer, listening. He knew he was not alone, but he didn't see anyone.

Suddenly, one of the shadows fledged a shape: a twisted gnome, bald, bearded, clad in leather; his eyes were red and his ears were hairy—and a gorgeous ring glittered on his finger.

"Who are you?" demanded Siegfried.

"A wise and kindly gnome who advises young heroes. My name is Regnir."

"What's a hero?"

"A warrior who knows no fear," said Regnir. "Whose spirit runs like fire through his veins, making him do more than mortal can."

"Like what?"

"Mostly he fights monsters, and seeks always for the ultimate monster—which is a dragon."

"And you advise these warriors? You?"

"I am more than I appear," said Regnir. "They come to me when young and I teach them some necessary magic. Because even heroes need a little extra help if they are to have any chance against monsters. I can read your mind, young sir, I can look right into the cauldron of dreams that lies behind your eyes and hear your unspoken question. You want to know whether you are of hero stock and whether I will help you."

"Wrong!" cried Siegfried. "I know what I am as far as I go, and how far I want to go. I have come to find a sword."

"Really? How do you know it's here?"

"A voice spoke in my sleep. It told me to dig beneath a singing tree."

"Singing tree? You mean a tree full of singing birds?"

"I don't know what I mean," said Siegfried. "But I'll find out."

They heard a chiming: "No bird, but me, me, me . . ."

"Look!" cried Siegfried. Regnir stared. Among all the trees clad in summer leaves stood a bare white birch sheathed in ice. Icicles clung to it, chiming like bells as a breeze passed through:

This is the glade,
this the tree.
Find the blade
and pull it free.

Siegfried snatched up a sharp stone, sprang at the tree, and began to dig. Regnir joined him. As we know, he could dig like a mole with his spade-shaped hands. He made the dirt fly. Digging together, they made a deep hole. Siegfried reached in and pulled something out. He stared at it. It was not a sword but a piece of broken metal—jagged, stained with corrosion.

"Pah!" he cried, and flung it to the ground.

"Not so fast," said Regnir. "Like me, it's better than it looks." He rubbed the metal with his sleeve. "See its color? See how blue it is? Not like any metal you've ever seen. This vein of blueness was dug out of a flaming mass of rock that fell out of the skies and made a hole in the earth. The Smith Dwarfs quarried the star metal, forged it into a dagger, and gave it to Odin as a gift. In his hands it tasted the blood of many a Giant and Ogre. Centuries later, Odin bestowed this dagger upon your father, who named it Blue-blade and used it as a sword—most honorably. But then, when he was treacherously attacked and on the point of death, he broke the sword so that no enemy would take it, and your mother, before she died, buried this piece under the tree."

"It's still not a sword," growled Siegfried. "I can't use it as it is, despite its pedigree."

"If I teach you how to make it into a sword again," said Regnir, "will you do something for me?"

"Do what?"

"Fight a dragon who stole my gold."

"Gladly," cried Siegfried. "Of course! Restore to me my father's sword and I shall use it against any monster you wish."

"Very well," said Regnir. "You must come with me now to the underground workshop of the Smith Dwarfs. They will show you how to temper the metal and reforge it into the very likeness of the sword that a hero father would pass on to a hero son."

"Let's go!" cried Siegfried. "Give me hammer and fire and the wit to work well! Let's go, let's go!"

13

Hero and Dragon

The river-bred youth who could endure any hardship in the open air, or in the water, or in snow and ice, almost choked to death in the sooty chamber that was the underground workshop of the Smith Dwarfs. The dwarfs stared in wonder as he gasped over his anvil, trying to breathe, the broad keg of his chest pumping like a bellows. The little smiths couldn't understand it. They breathed charcoal dust as if it were purest mountain air.

But Siegfried was determined not to give in. Exerting his will as though it were a separate muscle, he taught himself to draw the soot into his lungs without choking, and to extract oxygen from it as a fish uses its gills to take air out of water. And, gradually, he learned to work metal.

Now, indeed, the gnomes gaped in amazement, watching him drive a hole into a boulder-sized lump of iron and insert a shaft of wood that seemed as long as a mast. Wielding this enormous sledge, he seemed to the dwarfs like Thor descended, swinging his divine hammer.

Siegfried laid his blade on the anvil and beat it smooth. Using a pair of iron tongs, he lifted the blade off the anvil and held it in the fire until it glowed red-hot—kept holding it there until it turned into a bolt of quivering white fire. Then he plunged the white-hot blade into a bucket of melted snow. Steam hissed from the bucket, a great gout of steam, filling the chamber, and drifting out through crannies of rock, frightening folk in the valley below who thought that the old dead volcano was about to erupt.

The blade was star-blue again when Siegfried drew it out of the bucket. The lad respected the skill of the Smith Dwarfs and had done everything according to their instructions. Only now in the last instance did he reject their advice. For after they had pronounced the blade well-tempered and ready to be fitted with a hilt and receive its final exquisite honing, Siegfried surprised them by refusing to let the iron, bowl-shaped hilt be filigreed with silver, as they wished, or coated in gold leaf. He demanded that it be covered with melted lead. They argued with him, pointing out that a lead-covered hilt would be heavy, awkward, throwing off the entire balance of the sword.

He listened, smiling, but insisted on his own way. He himself regretted the balance of the sword being flawed by its leaden hilt, but he thought he had a good reason for doing as he had done.

For he had watched the smiths melting lead in small iron ladles as they made molds for gold work, and had studied the way the heavy metal turned to liquid, how it ran and spread. Watching it, he had felt an idea quicken. He had turned the idea over and over, examining it on all sides, then decided that the hilt be coated with lead.

By the time he left the smithy, all the dwarfs loved him. They made him promise to return for a week each year and swing his great mallet and make the mountain rumble.

The cave that held the stolen hoard opened onto a cliff overhanging a gray elbow of North Sea. Whales sounded here. Seals swarmed the beaches. Migrating reindeer passed. Wolves hunted

Clad in the pelt of a white wolf . . . Siegfried prowled about the treasure cave, studying Fafnir's habits.

the reindeer. South-ranging polar bears hunted the seals and walrus. Fafnir hunted them all.

Only nine days had passed since the night of the Hunters' Moon, and yellow leaves still hung on the trees. But snow was deepening on the slopes. Clad in the pelt of a white wolf so that he might not be visible against the snow, Siegfried prowled about the treasure cave, studying Fafnir's habits.

After shuffling many ideas and discarding them, Siegfried

finally came up with a plan. "I don't really like it," he said to himself. "It offers one chance in a thousand, maybe less. But I can't seem to think of anything better."

He had observed that Fafnir left the cave in the early afternoon and went down to the sea to hunt. On his way down, he flew through a narrow pass between two peaks. It was Siegfried's plan to conceal himself halfway down the slope on a ledge that jutted from the mountain, and when the dragon passed over him, to leap up, stabbing his sword upward, to pierce a spot under the jawbone where a great artery pulsed.

"It's a very vulnerable spot in humans," Siegfried said to himself. "You can fell the biggest, strongest man by pressing there with your thumb. But I'm not at all sure that it's a practical way to approach a dragon. Oh well, if it doesn't work I'll be meeting my father soon. Or will I? They say that dead heroes dine in Odin's hall, so he'll be there all right. He was a genuine hero—had a string of victories before he was put out of action. But I wonder whether being killed by a dragon will qualify me for Valhalla. Death by dragon is a decent way to go, of course, but a lifetime record of no victories and one defeat isn't too impressive. Enough of this. If I have only one chance in a thousand, that makes it a rare chance, doesn't it? So let me take it in good heart."

And, seeing the shadow of wings print themselves on the snow, he crouched, preparing to leap.

But the dragon, spotting movement on the ledge, spat a bit of fire, just enough to melt the snow and start a cascade of water tumbling down the mountain. Whatever he had seen, thought Fafnir, would be killed by the fall, and he could examine it when he landed.

Siegfried felt himself caught in the cascade, hurtling down. His boyhood in the Rhine, however, had taught him to ride an icy waterfall like a spawning salmon. He landed unhurt on the beach, and, seeing Fafnir drop toward him, dived into the sea and sped away.

Having seen how fast Siegfried could swim, Fafnir did not follow him into the water, but hovered on great leathery wings, spitting fire until he saw the water beginning to steam. Siegfried, feeling the heat, dived deep, then lanced down, down. . . . The water was very cold at this depth but he felt it warming and knew that the dragon was still skimming the surface, blowing flame.

Indeed, Fafnir was hovering over the spot where he had last seen Siegfried. He dipped down and blew another puff of flame, and watched the water boil. Fish bobbed to the surface and floated belly-up. Fafnir kept spitting fire, thinking, "I'll boil 'em all, including that pesky little would-be hero. I'll turn this

Fafnir lashed his spiked tail, trying to crush him
where he stood. Siegfried swung his sword . . .

whole damned bay into a chowder and lap it up at my leisure."

Siegfried, inching along the sea bottom, felt the frigid depths heating up. "I'll have to surface," he thought, "and let him catch me, or he'll kill every living thing in here and stink up the whole Northland. Well, if he swallows me he swallows my sword, and that may give him a monster bellyache."

And he began to swim up toward the surface. But he felt the water sway as a huge darkness passed him, and saw that a whale, made uneasy by the warming water, was preparing to broach. Swimming as fast as he could, Siegfried cut through the murk, reached the whale, and scrambled up its slippery side. He perched on its head as it ploughed toward the surface.

The whale broached. Siegfried clung desperately as it rose in the air and arched, falling toward the water again. He slid along its head until he was lying over the blowhole. The whale splashed down, bobbed up, and spouted. It shot out a jet of water with terrific force. Siegfried rode the spouting column, up, up—and saw the dragon rising after him, jaws wide, ready to catch him as he fell and swallow him whole.

The lad drew his sword, turned in the air, and fell toward the gaping jaws. He cocked his arm and hurled his sword hilt-first; he saw it enter Fafnir's maw.

And now, the fire inside the dragon's gullet melted the hilt. The hot lead spilled down the monster's throat and began to scorch its entrails. Screaming with pain, writhing in the air, threshing, Fafnir folded his wings and dropped into the water, trying to quench the agony that flamed in his guts. But the hot lead spread, scorching liver, lungs, intestines . . .

Siegfried hit the water and swam toward the beach—very fast, for Fafnir followed close. On the beach, the dragon faced Siegfried and slithered toward him. Belching smoke, the beast spat out the sword. Siegfried snatched up the charred blade and flung himself to the sand as Fafnir lashed his spiked tail, trying to crush him where he stood.

Siegfried swung his sword and sheared off the dragon's tail. Black blood gushed out. The lad leaped aside so that the blood

*The lad leaped aside so that the blood would not
splatter him, and swung his sword again.*

would not splatter him, and swung his sword again. The blade
sheared through the armored hide, through fat, muscle, tendons,
and thick bone, making the great lizard head seem to leap off its
shoulders. But the head, falling, retained enough murderous vitality to snap once more, biting off Siegfried's hand at the wrist.

Moving faster than thought, using his sword as a wedge,
Siegfried forced the dead jaws open and plunged the bleeding
stump of his wrist into the fiery gullet. He felt unbelievable pain
as the fire seared his raw stump. But he knew that the flame was
sealing the arteries, cleaning the wound, and preventing him from

*The head, falling, retained enough murderous vitality to
snap once more, biting off Siegfried's
hand at the wrist.*

bleeding to death. Nevertheless, the agony almost made him swoon. But a sweetness of triumph swept over him, giving him strength enough to bear the pain.

"I'll go back to the smithy," he thought, "and have the dwarfs make me a new hand, cunningly sinewed with copper wire. They will welcome such a task and do it well. Then I'll test their work by using the hand to finish what I have to do here."

Regnir waited impatiently while Siegfried visited the smithy. For the gnome was in debt now to the young hero, and had found that the most agreeable way to pay a debt was to kill the creditor.

And, since he had promised Siegfried half his treasure as a reward for meeting the dragon, he could not rest while Siegfried was still alive.

He did not waste time while waiting. He went to his garden and picked certain herbs. Now these herbs could be used as spices or poison according to the way Regnir prepared them and what spells he muttered while grinding and mixing. He brewed a poison that hissed and bubbled and began to eat its way through the thick stone crock. Regnir poured cold cow's milk in and the poison stopped bubbling, but still frothed about its edges.

"Doesn't matter," said Regnir to himself. "It looks creamy this way. He'll be very hot from the forge fires—and still scorched here and there, no doubt, by dragon-fire—and will gratefully gulp down what I offer. And it will eat big holes in his belly, and he'll be dead before he can take a second swallow."

Indeed, as Siegfried approached the bone house he saw Regnir waiting before the door, holding a big stone crock.

"Greetings, young hero!" cried Regnir. "All praise for your great victory!"

"Thank you," said Siegfried.

"You have come to collect your fee, no doubt," said Regnir. "But before we talk business let's have a cool drink together."

And he offered the crock.

Siegfried did not take it. "Look," he said, "see my new hand?"

"Very fine," muttered Regnir. "Splendid piece of work. Here, drink the milk before it gets warm."

"You drink first," said Siegfried.

"No, no, no!" cried Regnir. "You're the guest. You must drink first."

"But you're older," said Siegfried gently. "And worthy of special consideration. And those who raised me taught me absolute courtesy. Drink!"

Regnir drew back his arm, preparing to hurl the poison at

The Rhine-maidens began singing when they saw Siegfried. . . .

Siegfried's face, knowing that even a spatter would strip flesh from bone. But Siegfried's new iron hand shot out, gripped Regnir's neck and squeezed. The gnome's face bloated, grew purple; his eyes bulged, his mouth opened. Siegfried took the crock from his hand, then, tilting Regnir's face up, he poured the brew into his mouth—and sprang back as the gnome shriveled, blackened, fell to a mound of fuming dust.

Siegfried did not linger at the bone house. He climbed to the cave and helped himself to the hoard of gold—which he did not keep, but took back to the Rhine and returned to its original hiding place.

The Rhine-maidens began singing when they saw him come. They hadn't sung a note all the time he was gone. Now they blazed with joy and didn't want him to waste time with the hoard.

"Don't put it back," cried Arla. "Keep it. You won it. It's yours."

"No," said Siegfried. "What care I for this weight of metal? Let's stuff it back in its hole where it belongs. You are the true Rhine treasure, my golden girls! And I've come back to marry you."

"One at a time or all three?" they chorused.

"Both," he said.

Screaming with glee, they flung themselves on him and whirled him into a dance. It was Midsummer Eve and a yellow moon hung low. They danced until the sun paled and the stars dwindled and the dawn birds sang. And they were so wrapped in love and pleasure that any thief who might have happened by that night would have been able to steal the gold without any trouble at all.

And Urd and Loki were chuckling as they watched from above. For Siegfried with his courage, his wild innocence, and his carelessness of gain was, without knowing it, plaiting strands in their fatal web.

Thus, despite his joy that Midsummer Eve, Siegfried could not stay with the Rhine-maidens. For he had taken the cursed ring from Regnir and now wore it on his own finger, and felt other perils beckon.

All this happened long ago, long, long ago—before we began to doubt magic and diminish heroes. So long ago that it seems like a fading dream, or one of Loki's lies trying to come true.

Acknowledgments

Letter Cap Illustrations by Hrana L. Janto

Cover, FAFNIR *(1989) by Hrana Janto*
  Courtesy of the artist

Opposite page 1, HUMAN SKULL & BONE ROSETTE *(ca. 1540), in cathedral catacomb, Lima, Peru*
    Photo: Dennis Ryan Kelly, Jr., Indianapolis

Page 3, WATER *by Giuseppe Arcimboldo (1527–93), oil on canvas*
    Courtesy of the Kunsthistoriches Museum, Vienna
      Photo: Saskia/Art Resource, NY

Page 5, RAPE AND THEFT OF THE RED RABBIT *(1984) by Emilio Cruz, oil on canvas (7' × 7')*
    Courtesy of the artist

Page 8, WOTAN/ODIN IN SCENE FROM "DIE WALKÜRE" *(1914) by Franz Stassen, lithograph*
    Courtesy of the Nationalarchiv der Richard-Wagner-Stiftung/Richard-Wagner-Gedenkstätte, Bayreuth

Page 10, TEMPEST IN THE VALLEY OF AOSTA *by J. M. W. Turner (1775–1851), oil on canvas*
    Courtesy of the Art Institute of Chicago
      Photo: Scala/Art Resource, NY

Page 13, RHINE MAIDENS *(1914) by Franz Stassen, lithograph*
    Courtesy of the Nationalarchiv der Richard-Wagner-Stiftung/Richard-Wagner-Gedenkstätte, Bayreuth

Page 14, TALLADEGA THREE II *(1982) by Frank Stella, relief print (66" × 52"), signed edition of thirty, printed and published by Tyler Graphics Ltd. © Copyright Frank Stella and Tyler Graphics Ltd. 1982.*
    Courtesy of the artist and Tyler Graphics Ltd.

Page 19, THE FLY *(1988) by Earl Staley, acrylic on canvas board (8" × 10")*
    Courtesy of the artist
      Photo: Sarah Lewis

Page 20, A FLEET OF VIKING SHIPS IN A ROUGH SEA *by Edward Moran (1829–1901), oil on canvas*
    Photo: The Bettmann Archive, NY

Page 22, LAST VOYAGE OF THE DEAD *(ca. 1000), Viking carved rock*
    Courtesy of the Stockholm Museum
      Photo: Giraudon/Art Resource, NY

Page 24, *Detail from* VIKING SAGA *(ca. 1000), Viking carved rock*
    Courtesy of the Stockholm Museum
        Photo: Giraudon/Art Resource, NY

Page 26, BEAR HOLDING A SALMON *(19th century), ornament from a chief's headdress, Tsimshian tribe, British Columbia*
    Courtesy of the Metropolitan Museum of Art, the Michael C. Rockefeller Memorial Collection, Bequest of Nelson A. Rockefeller, 1979 (1979.206.443)

Page 29, HIDING FROM THE TAX MAN (FOREST) *(1986) by John Alexander, oil on canvas (90" × 100")*
    Courtesy of the artist and Marlborough Gallery, NY

Page 32, STILL LIFE *by Pablo Picasso (1881–1973), oil on canvas*
        Photo: Art Resource, NY

Page 40, ALBERICH CURSING WOTAN AND LOGE *(1914) by Franz Stassen, lithograph for Wagner's "*DAS RHEINGOLD.*"*
        Photo: Archiv für Kunst und Geschichte, Berlin

Page 44, RUBEZAHL *by Moritz von Schwind (1804–71), oil on canvas (25 3/8" × 15 3/4")*
    Courtesy of the Schack-Galerie, Munich
        Photo: Joachim Blauel/Artothek, Munich

Page 48, THE CLOWN, CABACILLAS *by Diego Velazquez (1599–1660), oil on canvas*
    Courtesy of the Prado, Madrid
        Photo: Scala/Art Resource, NY

Page 51, *Detail from* BENEFICENT RAIN *by Chang Yu-Tsai (d. 1316), Chinese hand scroll, ink on silk (h. 10 5/8" l. 106 3/4")*
    Courtesy of the Metropolitan Museum of Art, Gift of Douglas Dillon, 1985 (1985.227.2)

Page 52, *Hilt detail from Viking sword (ca. 10th century), iron, copper, and silver (l. overall 37 3/4" gr.w. 4 5/16" wt. 36 oz.)*
    Courtesy of the Metropolitan Museum of Art, Rogers Fund, 1955 (55.46.1)

Page 56, WATERFALLS OF REICHENBACH *by J. M. W. Turner, watercolor on paper on wood (21 1/2" × 21 1/8")*
    Courtesy of the Cecil Higgins Art Gallery, Belford
        Photo: Giraudon/Art Resource

Page 59, CHILD IN THE MEADOW, *detail from* MORNING *by Philipp Otto Runge (1777 1810), oil on canvas (60 7/8" × 45 1/8")*
    Courtesy of Kunsthalle, Hamburg
        Photo: Ralph Kleinhempel

Page 62, ALBERICH AND THE RHINE MAIDENS *(1876), colored woodcut of drawing by Knut Eckwall for Bayreuth production of Richard Wagner's "Das Rheingold."*
    Photo: Archiv für Kunst und Geschichte, Berlin

Page 64, OSSIAN'S DREAM *by Jean-Auguste-Dominique Ingres (1780–1867), oil on canvas*
    Courtesy of Musée Ingres, Montauban
        Photo: Giraudon/Art Resource, NY

Page 68, *Runic stone with a deity and inscription (ca. 800–900)*
    Courtesy of the Moesgard Museum, Denmark
        Photo: D.Y./Art Resource, NY

Page 72, IN THE FOREST (THE YOUTH'S MAGIC HORN) *(ca. 1848) by Moritz von Schwind, oil on canvas (19½" × 15½")*
  Courtesy of the Schack-Galerie, Munich
    Photo: Joachim Blauel/Artothek, Munich

Page 74, MARY, MARY SOLITARY *(1984) by Mary Armstrong, oil on panel (24" × 30")*
  Courtesy of the artist

Page 78, SIEGFRIED FORGING HIS SWORD *(1914) by Franz Stassen, lithograph*
  Courtesy of the Nationalarchiv der Richard-Wagner-Stiftung/Richard-Wagner-Gedenkstätte, Bayreuth

Page 81, SIEGFRIED *(ca. 1900), from a painting by Ferdinand Leeke*
  Courtesy of the Nationalarchiv der Richard-Wagner-Stiftung/Richard-Wagner-Gedenkstätte, Bayreuth

Page 83, SIEGFRIED BATTLING GIANT DRAGON *(1914) by Franz Stassen, lithograph*
  Courtesy of the Nationalarchiv der Richard-Wagner-Stiftung/Richard-Wagner-Gedenkstätte, Bayreuth

Page 85, SIEGFRIED *(1880) by K. Dielitz*
    Photo: Archiv für Kunst und Geschichte, Berlin

Page 86, SIEGFRIED AND FAFNIR *(ca. 1900) from a painting by H. Hendrich*
  Courtesy of the Nationalarchiv der Richard-Wagner-Stiftung/Richard-Wagner-Gedenkstätte, Bayreuth

Page 89, SIEGFRIED AND THE RHINE MAIDENS *by Alfred Pinkham Ryder (1847–1917), oil on canvas*
  Courtesy of the National Gallery of Art, Washington, D.C.
    Photo: Art Resource, NY

BOOKS BY BERNARD EVSLIN

Merchants of Venus
Heroes, Gods and Monsters of the Greek Myths
Greeks Bearing Gifts: The Epics of Achilles and Ulysses
The Dolphin Rider
Gods, Demigods and Demons
The Green Hero
Heraclea
Signs & Wonders: Tales of the Old Testament
Hercules
Jason and the Argonauts